SRA Open Court Reading

Bev Travels

A Division of The McGraw-Hill Companies

Columbus, Ohio

www.sra4kids.com

SRA/McGraw-Hill
A Division of The **McGraw·Hill** *Companies*

Copyright © 2002 by SRA/McGraw-Hill.

All rights reserved. Except as permitted under the United States Copyright Act, no part of this publication may be reproduced or distributed in any form or by any means, or stored in a database or retrieval system, without prior written permission from the publisher.

Printed in the United States of America.

Send all inquiries to:
SRA/McGraw-Hill
8787 Orion Place
Columbus, OH 43240-4027

ISBN 0-07-569732-7
 2 3 4 5 6 7 8 9 DBH 05 04 03 02

This is Bev. Bev likes to travel.

Bev does not drive, but she goes all over.
Bev's pals marvel at her tales.

This time Bev hides in a van.

The van is Evan's van.

Vic is Evan's cat.

Bev quivers! Bev's travel plans have just unraveled!

Practice Book 55 Bev Travels

Previously Introduced High-Frequency Words
a
is
on
the
an
in
was
are
and
I
make
makes
by
down
too
who
can
no
there
where
with
does
for
he
what
yes
have
puts
said
she
to
get
gets
so
wants
pulls
after
first
new
old
put
were
her
laugh
my
of
out
will
would
work
you
do

here
one
start
started
be
like
from
good
made
went
play
five
four
three
two
into
see
think
both
sees
wish
asked
away
how
me
your
ride
they
want
we
white
little
now
been
could
laughed
live
very
worked
over
go
going
around
eating
look
saw
some
together
being
give
use
please
once
read
goes

again
gives
looks
today

Sound-Spelling Correspondences in Decodable Books
1. /s/ spelled *s*;
   /m/ spelled *m*;
   /a/ spelled *a*;
   /t/ spelled *t*
2. /h/ spelled *h_*
3. /p/ spelled *p*
4. /i/ spelled *i*
5. /n/ spelled *n*
6. /l/ spelled *l*
7. *ll, all*
8. /d/ spelled *d*
9. /o/ spelled *o*
10. /b/ spelled *b*
11. /k/ spelled *c*
12. /k/ spelled *_ck*
13. /r/ spelled *r*
14. /u/ spelled *u*
15. /g/ spelled *g*
16. /j/ spelled *j*
17. /j/ spelled *_dge*
18. /f/ spelled *f*
19. /or/ spelled *or*
20. /e/ spelled *e*
21. /d/, /t/ spelled *ed*
22. /f/ spelled *_ff*;
    Review
23. /ks/ spelled *_x*
24. /z/ spelled *z*
25. /z/ spelled *_zz*
26. /z/ spelled *_s*
27. /e/ spelled *_ea_*
28. /s/ spelled *_ss*
29. /sh/ spelled *sh*; *es* ending
30. /th/ spelled *th*
31. Schwa
32. /ch/ spelled *ch*
33. /ch/ spelled *_tch*
34. /ar/ spelled *ar*
35. /m/ spelled *mb*
36. /w/ spelled *w_*
37. /hw/ spelled *wh_*
38. /er/ spelled *er*
39. /er/ spelled *ir*
40. /er/ spelled *ur*
41. /l/ spelled *le*
42. /l/ spelled *el*
43. /k/ spelled *k*
44. /ng/ spelled *_ng*
45. /kw/ spelled *qu_*
46. /y/ spelled *y_*
47. /ā/ spelled *a*
48. /ā/ spelled *a_e*
49. /s/ spelled *ce*
50. /s/ spelled *ci_*
51. /ī/ spelled *i*
52. /ī/ spelled *i_e*
53. /ō/ spelled *o*
54. /ō/ spelled *o_e*
55. /v/ spelled *v*

Bev Travels

Level 1
Practice Book 55

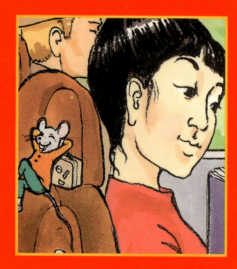

www.sra4kids.com

A Division of The McGraw·Hill Companies